About the Author

Irene Daria, Ph.D. is a developmental psychologist who specializes in teaching children how to read.

In addition to teaching the children of many celebrities to read, she has taught hundreds of other children—both as a paid specialist and as a volunteer—and has trained teachers in the science of reading.

A passionate literacy advocate, Dr. Daria is the founder and director of Steps Tutoring in New York City. Her *Steps to Reading* workbook series will enable you to teach a child how to read using the same research-based, fun, and effective methods Dr. Daria uses in her renown private lessons.

For more information, visit:
www.StepsTutoring.com or www.StepstoReading.com.

Bulk discounts are available. Please email: info@StepsPublishing.com

For more information about this series of workbooks see:

www.StepstoReading.com

Copyright © 2024 by STEPS Publishing, Inc. All rights reserved. No part of this book may be reproduced or utilized in any form or by any electronic or mechanical means, including photocopying, without permission in writing from the publisher.

Printed in the U.S.A.
ISBN 978-0-9864329-7-2

Book 2

ST📦PS to...
Reading

by Irene Daria, Ph.D.

Illustrations by Tingting Wei, Eryka Sajek, and Eric Wiener

Table of Contents

Double consonants (twin letters)
Includes sight word: see .... Pg. 2

--ck at the end of a word
Includes sight word: says .... Pg. 12

Beginning Blends

Words that begin with sl
Includes sight words: go, no .... Pg. 28

Words that begin with cl, gl, fl, bl, pl
Includes sight word: down .... Pg. 38

Words that begin with st .... Pg. 50

Words that begin with sn, sp, sk, sm, sw
Includes sight words: pull, put, full.. Pg. 56

Words that begin with tr, cr, dr, gr, fr
Includes sight word: little .... Pg. 66

Ending Blends

Words that end in nd
Includes sight word: with .... Pg. 86

Words that end in mp or nk
Includes sight word: look .... Pg. 94

Words that end in ng, nt
Includes sight word: said .... Pg. 106

What this book teaches

This is Book 2 in the *Steps to Reading* series. The book begins by teaching words that end in double consonants (words like "hill" and "hiss') and words that end in "ck" (words like "kick" and "peck"). It then turns to its primary focus – teaching words that contain consonant blends. These are words in which two consonants at either the beginning or end of a word are both sounded out.

Children will first learn words that have blends at the beginning (words like "slip" and "stop"); then words with blends at the end (words like "hand" and "dump" and "tent"); then words that have blends at both the beginning and the end (words like "stamp" and "grand").

Book 2 builds on the short vowel skills taught in Book 1. "Short" refers to the sounds vowels make in words like "cat," "him," "bus," "hen," and "hot." If your student has not yet mastered the short vowel sounds, it is a good idea to complete *Steps to Reading Book 1* before using this book.

Supplemental materials

The books listed below are great practice for the skills your student will be learning as he or she progresses through the lessons in this book. I highly recommend getting them when you begin this book because your student will be reading them very soon!

- "Jack and Jill and Big Dog Bill: A Phonics Reader," by Martha Weston. Published by Random House Books for Young Readers.
- "The Alphabet Series, Volume 1." This is a set of 18 little books published by Educators Publishing Service.
- "Now I'm Reading! Level One: Animal Antics." This is an e-book set of early readers by Nora Gaydos from Random House. There are several level one sets. Make sure you buy the one called "Animal Antics."
- "A Truck Can Help," by Judy Kentor Schmauss. This is part of the Reader's Clubhouse series of books published by Barron's.
- "Ducks in Muck," by Lori Haskins. Published by Random House Books for Young Readers.

Step 1   Twin letters

Twin letters make one sound.

Instructions

Say to the child: "**When 2 letters that are the same stand side-by-side, they make only one sound.**

"For example, in the word 'hill,' the 2 'l's make just one /l/ sound. In the word 'kiss,' the two 's's make just one /s/ sound."

Write a word

Say: "**Write 2 'l's on the blank lines and read the words out loud.**"

bi _ _	hi _ _
fi _ _	fe _ _
be _ _	Ji _ _
do _ _	pi _ _

Write the word and circle the picture

Say: "Read the word out loud. Then write the word, and circle the picture that shows the word."

hill

___ ___ ___ ___

doll

___ ___ ___ ___

kiss

___ ___ ___ ___

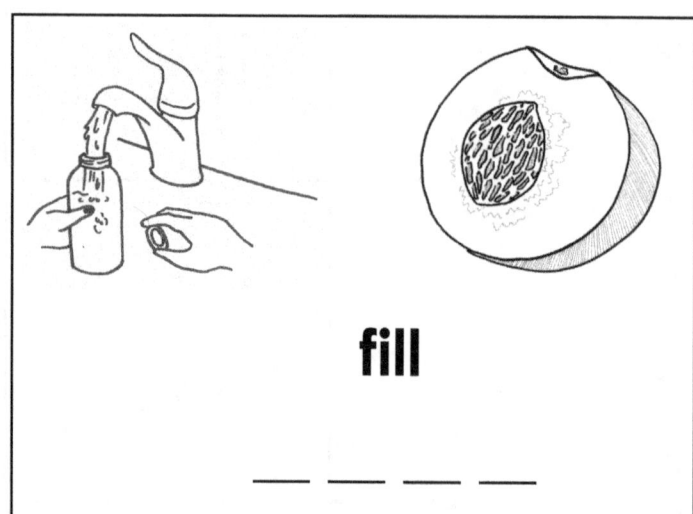

fill

___ ___ ___ ___

fell

___ ___ ___ ___

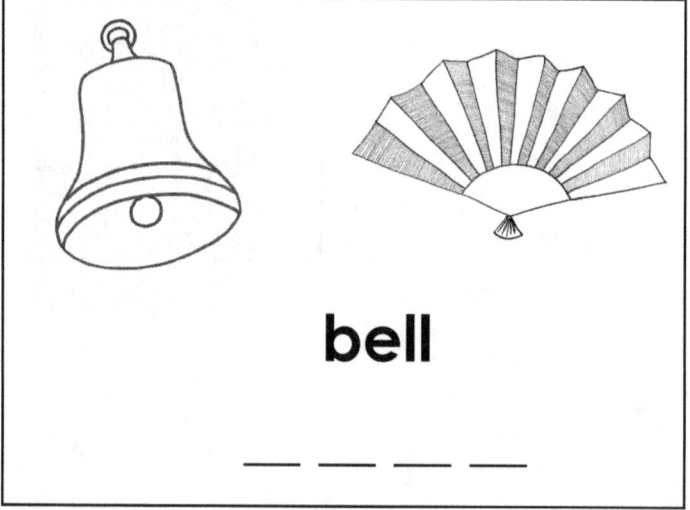

bell

___ ___ ___ ___

Circle the letters

Say: **"Circle the correct letters. Then write the word."**
Tell the child the pictures show: doll, kiss, hill, bell, fill, fell.

ⓓ m ⓞ p n ⓛ ⓛ t   d o l l

d k p i r s l s   _ _ _ _

h d f i g l s   _ _ _ _

b m e j l k l s   _ _ _ _

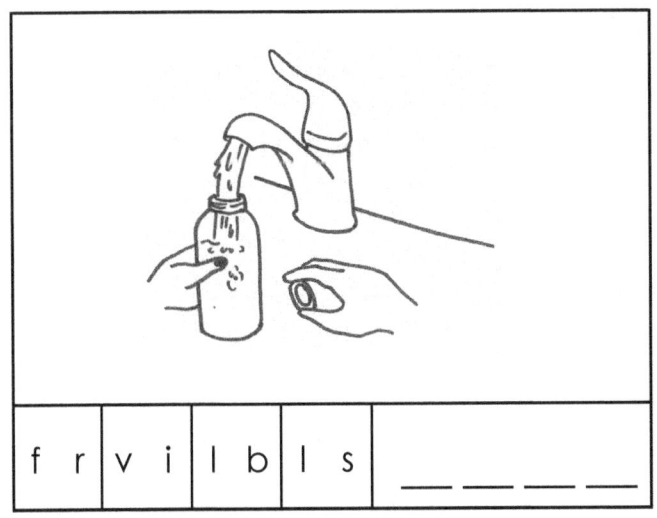

f r v i b l s   _ _ _ _

m f e h t l s l   _ _ _ _

5

Step 2

What you need to know about...
Sight Words

Sight Words are words the child needs to memorize, as opposed to sound out. Sight words either do not follow phonics rules (and, therefore, cannot be sounded out) or they are very common words that follow phonics rules the child has not yet learned.

The sight words in this book are presented in the order they will appear in the stories children will be reading as they make their way through this book. I call them Power Words because knowing how to read these sight words will increase the child's reading power. Since these words are so common in stories, memorizing them will enable your child to read many books much more quickly.

If your student completed *Steps to Reading Book 1*, then he or she knows the 12 most common sight words. (They are listed on the opposite page.) If your student did not complete Book 1, make sure your student knows these words before proceeding.

First set of Power Words

This is a summary of the Power Words the child should know at this point.

the	has	off
is	to	his
on	was	dog
as	of	for

Power Word

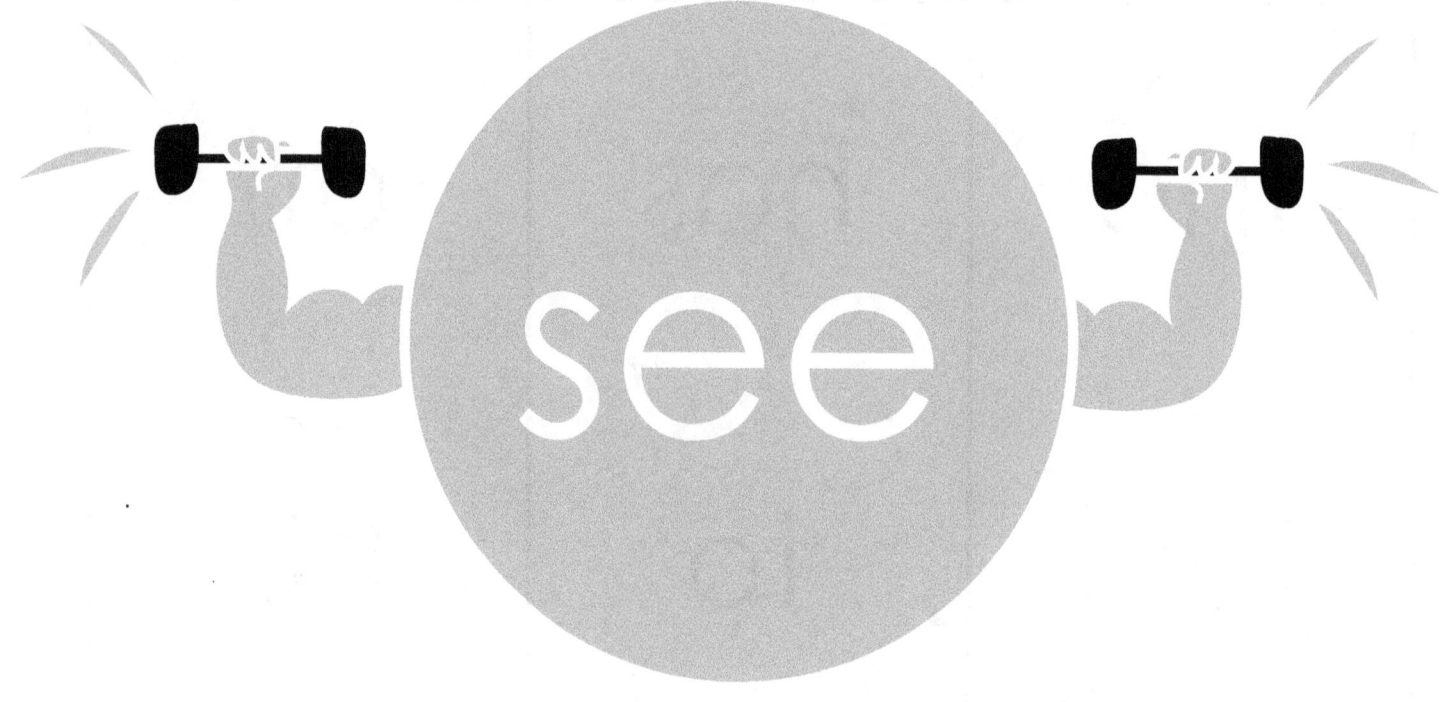

Instructions

1. Say: "**Some words don't follow any of the sounding-out rules. They are words that just need to be memorized. We will call them Power Words because they are words that appear very often in the stories you will be reading. Knowing these words will really boost your reading power.**"
2. Point to the word "see," *above.* Say, "**This word is 'see.'**"
3. Point to the word "see" on the top line on the opposite page. Say, "**Trace the word 'see.' Then write it four times next to the one you traced.**"
4. Repeat until the child has completed the whole sheet.
5. Any time you come to a Power Word lesson in this book, read the word to the child and have him or her trace and write the word on the lines that follow.

Write the Word

see

see

see

see

see

see

Does the sentence make sense?

Say: "**Read each sentence out loud. Color in the smiley face if the sentence makes sense and the frown if it does not.**"

	☺ ☹
I see a cat on the hill.	☺ ☹
I see the man has a wet hat.	☺ ☹
The dog did see the cat kiss the bell.	☺ ☹
I see Jill will fill the cup.	☺ ☹
The wet ham did see the bat.	☺ ☹
I see the log fell on the hill.	☺ ☹
Bill did see the bell kiss the doll.	☺ ☹
I see the doll will fill the hill.	☺ ☹

Read a book!

Instructions

Read a book

The child should read:

- "Oops! I See a Cat." This is the first book in the Alphabet Series. See "Supplemental Materials," p. 1.

Step 3

The sound of 'ck'

'ck' says
'k' as in truck

Instructions

Say to the child: "**The letters 'ck' say 'k' as in the words truck, pack, and luck.**"

Write a word

Say: **"Write 'ck' on the blank lines and read the words out loud."**

ba__	ki __
lo__	du__
de__	li __
pa__	si__

Write the word and circle the picture

Say: "Read the word out loud. Then write the word and circle the picture that shows the word."

tack

_ _ _ _

lick

_ _ _ _

duck

_ _ _ _

neck

_ _ _ _

sock

_ _ _ _

kick

_ _ _ _

Which word is it?

Say: "**Read each word out loud. Circle the word that goes with the picture.**"

rock   rack

sick   sack

tuck   tack

lock   lick

sock   sick

peck   pack

Draw a line from the word to the picture

Say: "**Read each word out loud.** Then draw a line from the correct word to the picture."

back pick sock 	lick sack kick 
neck tack tuck 	duck deck dock 
peck deck pick 	luck lock lick 

Circle the letters

Say: "**Circle the correct letters. Then write the word.**"
Tell the child the pictures show: sock, peck, kick, rock, tack, lock.

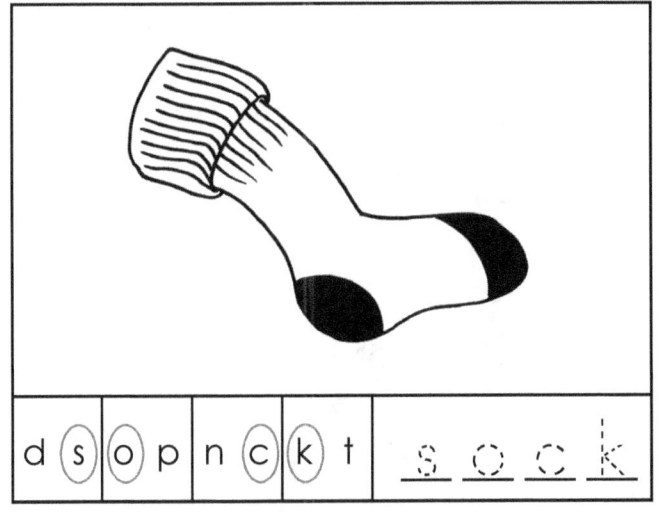

d (s) o p n (c) (k) t   s o c k

y p e w r c m k   _ _ _ _

k c o i c v l k   _ _ _ _

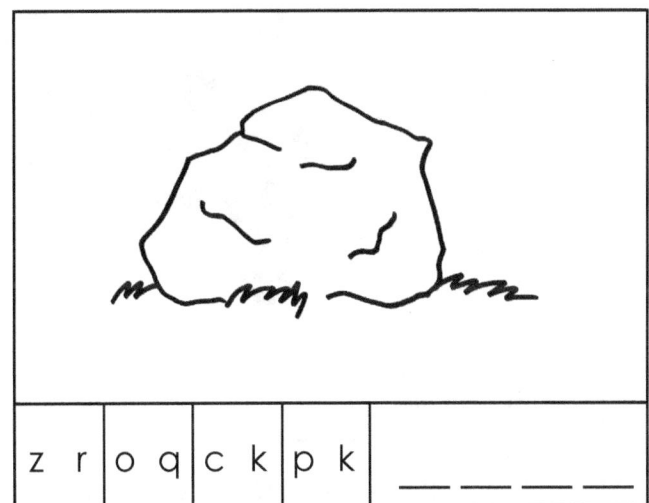

z r o q c k p k   _ _ _ _

s t a i c x u k   _ _ _ _

w l o h v c k r   _ _ _ _

17

Play Bingo with words that end in "ck"

Instructions

<u>Materials:</u>
- Flashcards. Cut out the cards on the opposite page.
- 2 gameboards follow the flashcards. In Bingo, every player gets his or her own gameboard. You and the child should each select a gameboard to use.
- Pennies to use as game pieces.

1. Place the flashcards in one stack, with the words facing up.
2. Have the child read the word on the top card in the stack.
3. Each of you should look for that word on your Bingo boards and place a penny on top of the word on your boards when you find it.
4. Place the card the child read face down on the table.
5. Repeat steps 2-4. The child should be the one doing all of the reading of the words on the flashcards. Continue until one of you has three pennies in a row, either horizontally, vertically, or diagonally. The first player to get three in a row should call out, "Bingo!" That player wins the game.

Bingo Flashcards

Cut out the cards along the dotted lines.

lick	tuck	duck
kick	back	sock
rock	pack	sick

This page is intentionally left blank.

This page is intentionally left blank.

BINGO

lick	tuck	duck
kick	back	sock
rock	pack	sick

BINGO

kick	lick	back
duck	rock	sock
pack	sick	tuck

This page is intentionally left blank.

Step 4   Power Word

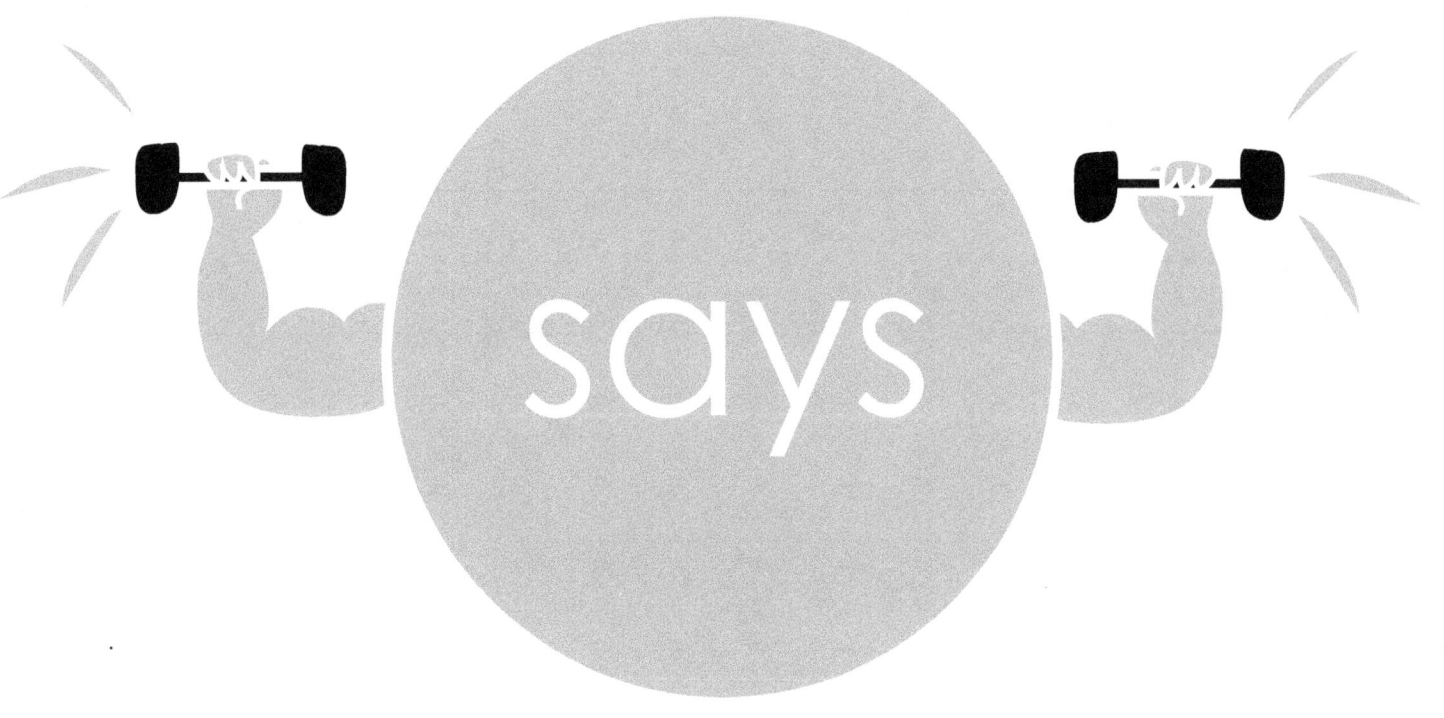

Instructions

Point to the word "says," *above*. Say, "**This word is `says' as in, `The boy says he can't come to the park today,' or `Mom always says, 'I love you.'"**

Write the Word

Say, "Trace the word 'says.' Then write it four times next to the one you traced."

says

says

says

says

says

says

Read a book!

Instructions

Read a book

The child should read:

- Jack and Jill and Big Dog Bill, by Martha Weston. See "Supplemental Materials," p. 1.

Note

Your student will be able to read most of the words in the story but there will be a few words the child has not learned yet. When you reach these words – such as "down" or "go" – read the words to the child. Tell the child he or she will be learning those new words in the next few lessons.

Step 5　　　　　　　　　　　　　　　Beginning Blends

Instructions

Say to the child: "**You are ready to move on to the next step in reading! You're going to be reading words that have two consonants in front of the vowel. Each of those consonants will make its own sound.**"

Words that begin with 'sl'

Words that begin with...

sl

Instructions
Say to the child: "**Look at the pictures, below. They show how adding just one letter makes a whole new word!**"

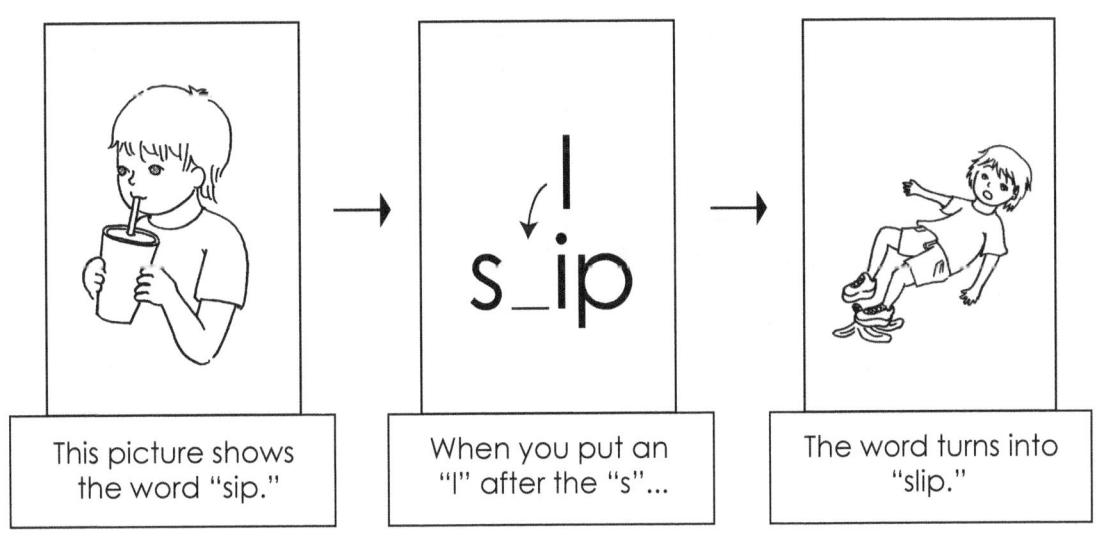

This picture shows the word "sip."

When you put an "l" after the "s"...

The word turns into "slip."

Write words that begin with sl–

Say: **"Write 'sl' on the blank lines and read the words out loud."**

__ip	__ap
__im	__am
__ed	__id
__ack	__ick

Which word is it?

Say: **"Read each word out loud. Circle the word that goes with the picture."**

slug   lug

slick   lick

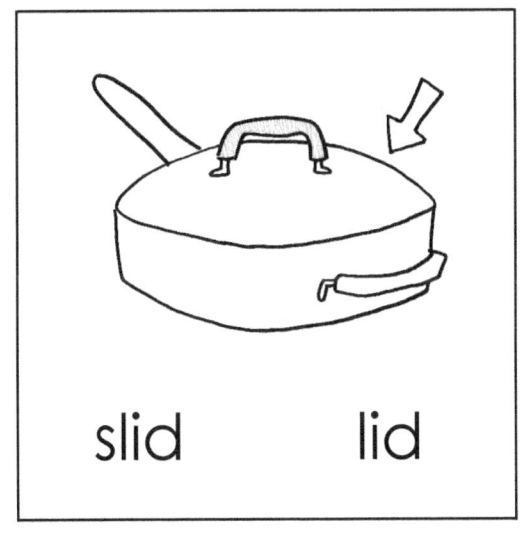

slid   lid

slam   Sam

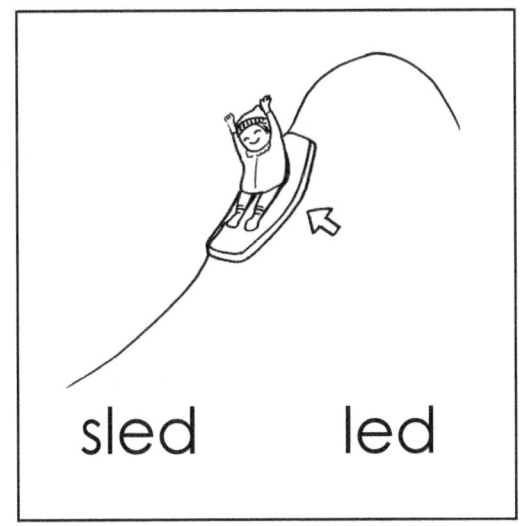

sled   led

slip   lip

Play the sl– board game

First one to reach the end wins!

Instructions

<u>Materials you will need</u>:
- A single die.
- Coins to use as markers.
- Gameboard, *opposite page*.

1. Each player places a coin on "start."
2. Take turns rolling the die.
3. Move forward the same amount of spaces as the number on the die.
4. As you move forward on the board, make the sound of the letters, or read the word, that you pass and land on.
5. For example, if a five comes up on the die, move five spaces on the game board and read five words and/or sounds.
6. The first person to reach the end wins.

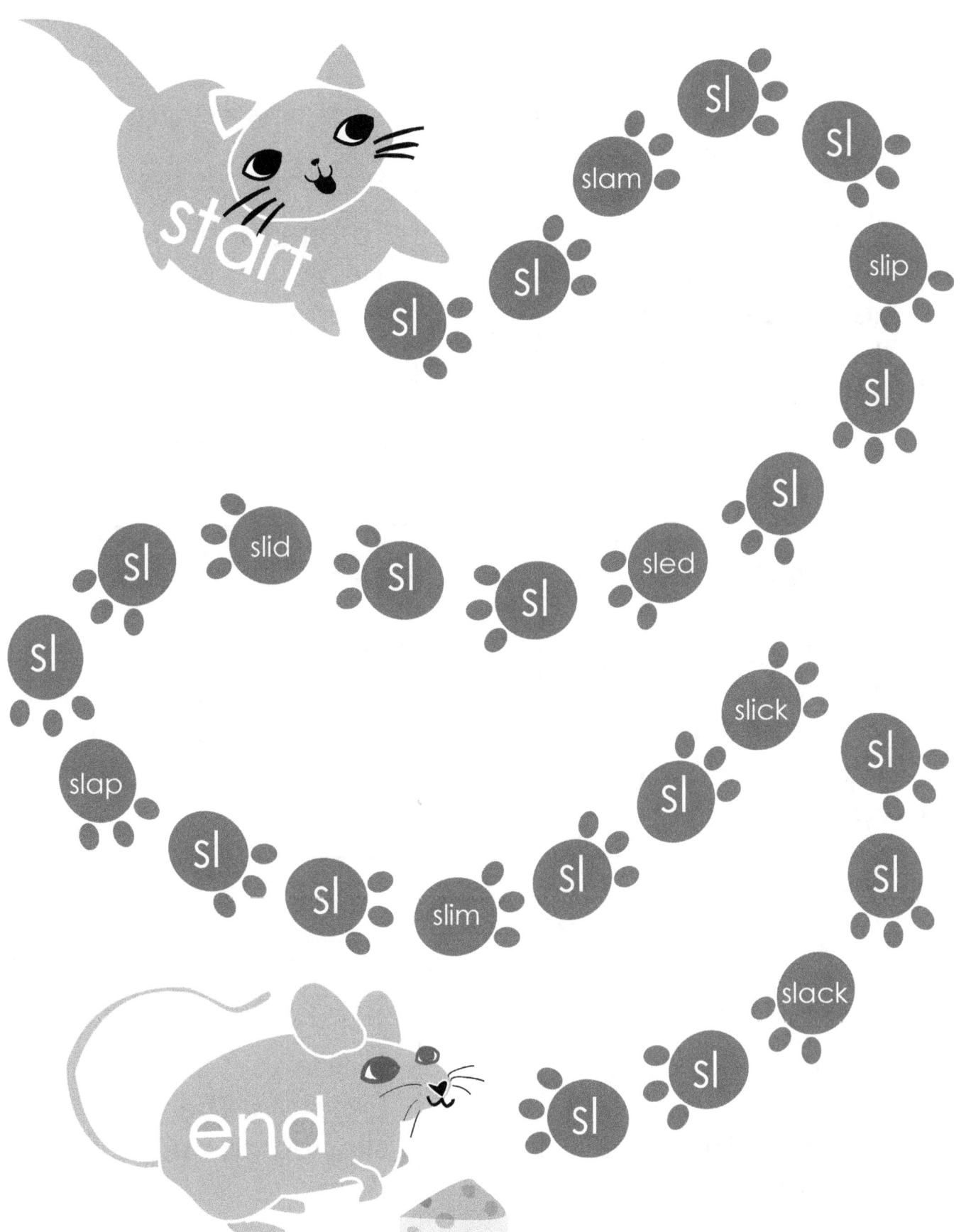

Vocabulary

tack
A small nail.
Example: **The tack held the edge of the paper on the bulletin board.**

peck
To bite, or hit, with a beak.
Example: **The bird pecked at the food.**

lug
To carry something heavy.
Example: **She will lug a stack of books up the stairs.**

slim
Small or thin.
Example: **The boy was very slim.**

slack
Loose, or not held tightly.
Example: **The rope was slack.**

slick
Slippery.
Example: **The girl slipped on the slick floor.**

Step 6   Power Words

Does the sentence make sense?

Say: "**Read each sentence out loud. Color in the smiley face if the sentence makes sense, and the frown if it does not.**"

	☺	☹
The duck will go lick the sock.		
The dog did not go up the hill.		
The duck will go peck the lock.		
A pig will go mess up the bed.		
The cat did go kiss his sock.		
I will go pet the dog.		
A duck did go slip on the sled.		
A dog did go fill the cup.		

Read a book!

Instructions

Read a book

The child can now read the following books in the Alphabet Series. See "Supplemental Materials," p. 1.

- Book 2: Tom at the Dam
- Book 3: Tim the Hog
- Book 4: Jim and Cal

Tip: The child should read just one book a day. Have the child reread each book until he or she can read it easily. Then move on to the next book.

Step 7

Words that begin with...

cl-, gl-, fl-, bl-, pl-

| Instructions |

Say to the child: "**You did a great job learning how to read words that begin with 'sl.' Now you will learn words that begin with cl-, gl-, fl-, bl-, pl-.**"

cl-, gl-, fl-, bl-, pl- words

Say: **"Circle the letters at the beginning of the word the picture shows."**
Tell the child the pictures show: clock, flag, block, glass, sled, and clap.

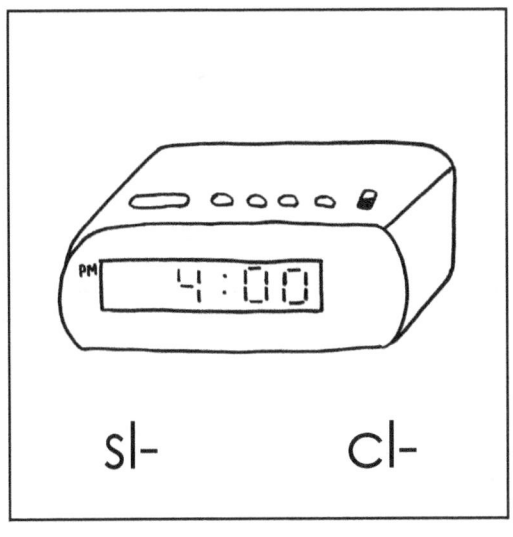

sl-   cl-

fl-   gl-

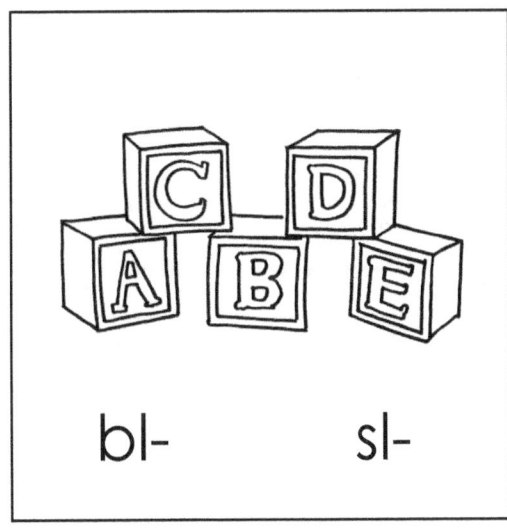

bl-   sl-

gl-   fl-

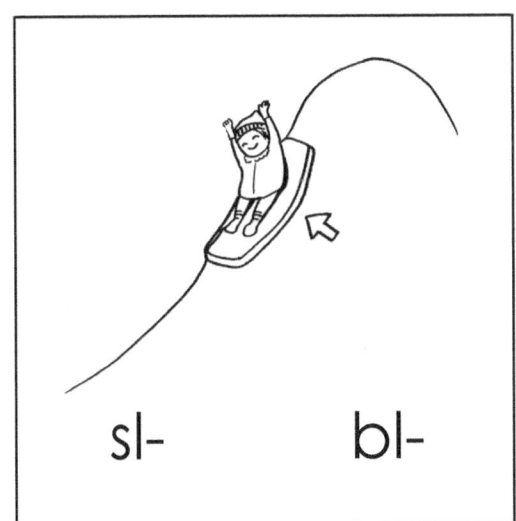

sl-   bl-

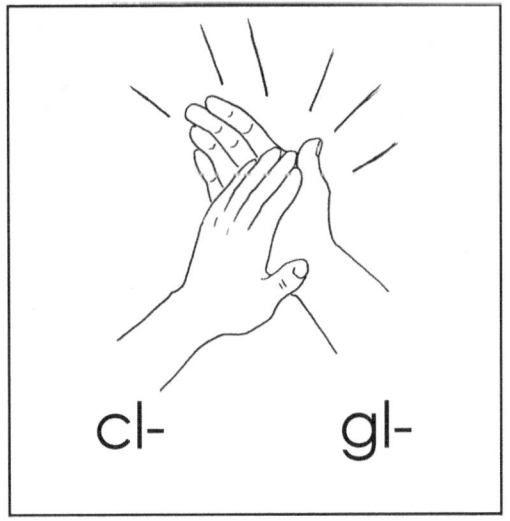

cl-   gl-

39

Write and read the word

Sound out ↓	Write the letter ↓	Write and read the word ↓
sl	s l ip	_ _ _ _
cl	_ _ ub	_ _ _ _
bl	_ _ ock	_ _ _ _ _
fl	_ _ ag	_ _ _ _
gl	_ _ ad	_ _ _ _
fl	_ _ ip	_ _ _ _
pl	_ _ um	_ _ _ _

Which word is it?

Say: "**Read each word out loud. Circle the word that goes with the picture.**"

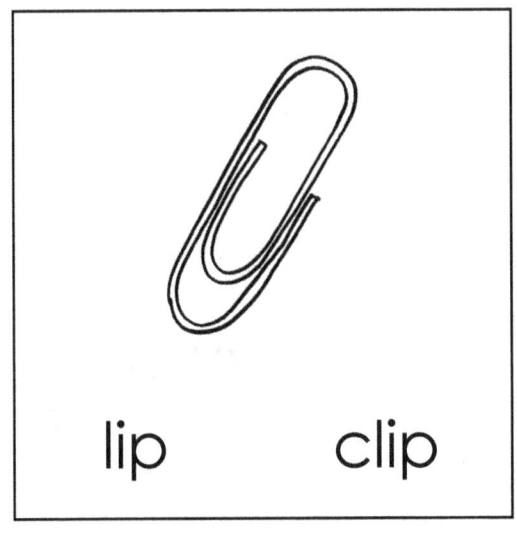

lip   clip

slick   lick

flag   lag

lock   block

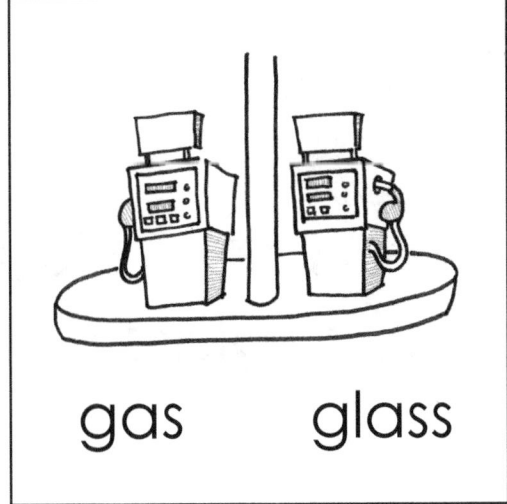

gas   glass

lap   clap

Write the word and circle the picture

Say: "Read the word out loud. Then write the word, and circle the picture that shows the word."

flag

___ ___ ___ ___

glad

___ ___ ___ ___

flat

___ ___ ___ ___

block

___ ___ ___ ___ ___

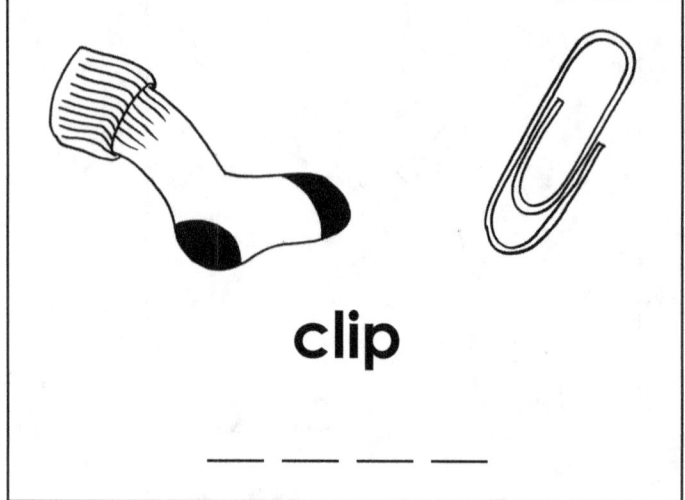

clip

___ ___ ___ ___

glass

___ ___ ___ ___ ___

Draw a line from the word to the picture

Say: "**Read each word out loud. Then draw a line from the correct word to the picture.**"

clap clip plum 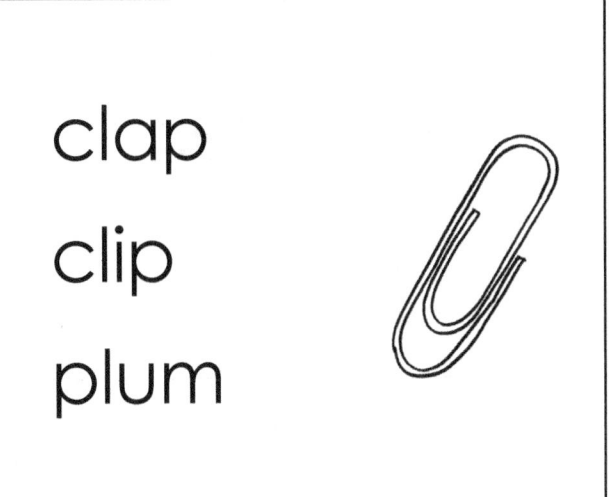	fat flat flag 
lick lock block 	block glad glass 
sled slip slam 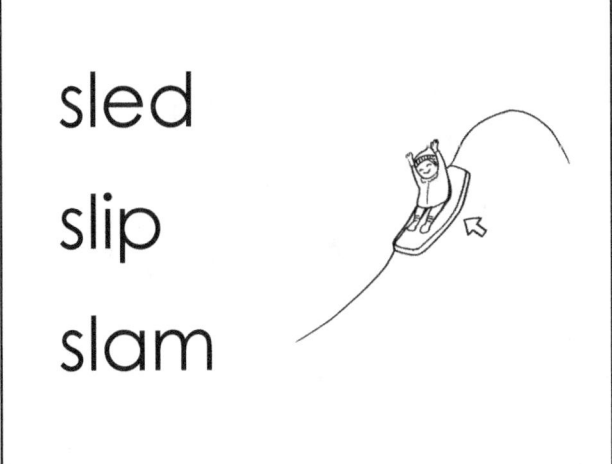	sock clock duck 

43

Circle the letters

Say: "**Circle the correct letters. Then write the word.**"
Tell the child the pictures show: clip, flag, flat, slip, glass, block.

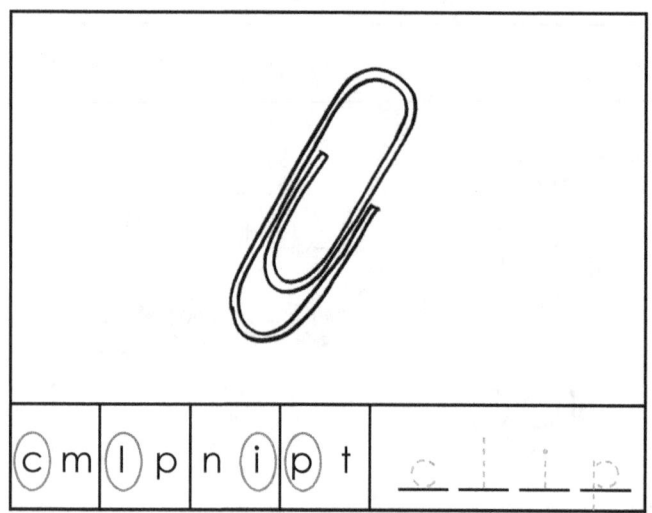

c m l p n i p t   c l i p

d f l i r a s g   _ _ _ _

h f l a i a t n   _ _ _ _

b s e l n i u p   _ _ _ _

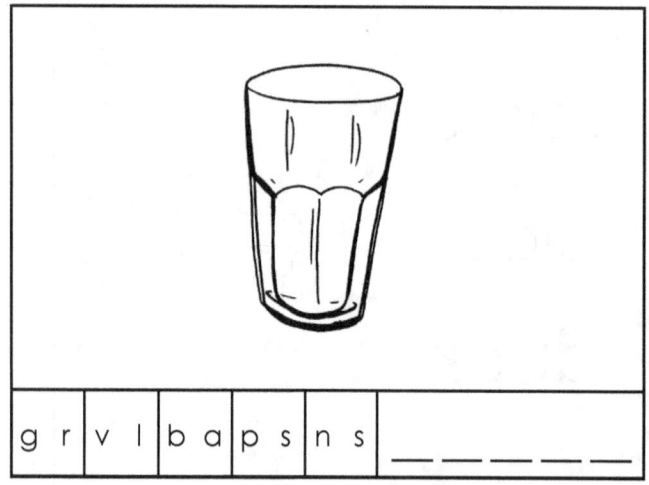

g r v l b a p s n s   _ _ _ _ _

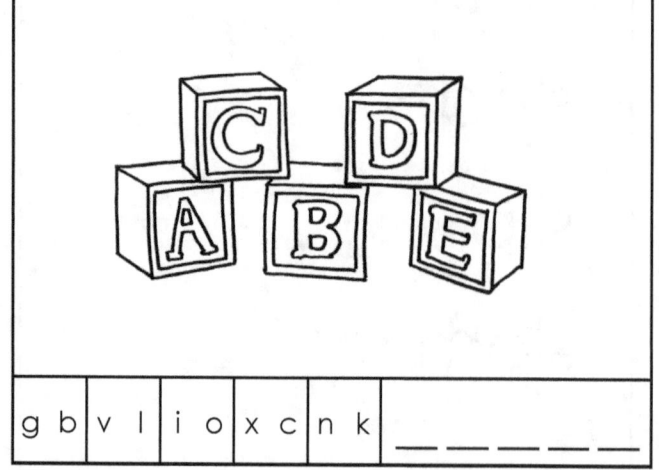

g b v l i o x c n k   _ _ _ _ _

Step 8   Power Word

down

down

down

down

Play a board game!

First one to reach the end wins!

Instructions

Materials you will need:
- A single die.
- Coins to use as markers.
- Gameboard, *opposite page*.

1. Each player places a coin on "start."
2. Take turns rolling the die.
3. Move forward the same amount of spaces as the number on the die.
4. As you move forward on the board, read the words that you pass and land on.
5. For example, if a five comes up on the die, move five spaces on the game board and read five words.
6. The first person to reach the end wins.

Does the sentence make sense?

Say: "**Read each sentence out loud. Color in the smiley face if the sentence makes sense, and the frown if it does not.**"

	☺ ☹
The slim pig did slip on the flag.	☺ ☹
The sled did go down the hill.	☺ ☹
A cat did see a duck pack a sack.	☺ ☹
The sled slid down on the slick sock.	☺ ☹
Jack and Jill sat down on the rock.	☺ ☹
The black cat will go down to the man.	☺ ☹
The duck did go down on the log.	☺ ☹
The cat did go down on the sled.	☺ ☹

Read a book!

Instructions

Read a book

The child can now read the following book in the "Now I'm Reading! Level One: Animal Antics," set by Nora Gaydos. See "Supplemental Materials," p. 1.
- Book 1: "Fat Cat"

Step 9

Instructions

Say to the child: **"You did a great job learning how to read words that have 'l' as the second letter. Now you will learn words that begin with 'st.'"**

st- or sl- ?

Say: " **Circle the letters at the beginning of the word the pictures show.**"
Tell the child the pictures show: sled, step, stop, slip, slam, stick.

Write and read the word

Sound out ↓	Write the letter ↓	Write and read the word ↓
st	s t em	_ _ _ _
st	_ _ ep	_ _ _ _
st	_ _ op	_ _ _ _
st	_ _ ill	_ _ _ _ _
st	_ _ ick	_ _ _ _ _
st	_ _ uck	_ _ _ _ _
st	_ _ uff	_ _ _ _ _

Read a book!

Instructions

Read a book

The child can now read the following book in the "Animal Antics" set by Nora Gaydos. See "Supplemental Materials," p. 1.

- Book 2: "Hot Dog"

Play "Stop and Clap"

First one to reach the end wins!

Instructions

Materials you will need:
- A single die.
- Coins to use as markers.
- Gameboard, *opposite page*.

1. Each player places a coin on "start."
2. Take turns rolling the die.
3. Move forward the same amount of spaces as the number on the die.
4. As you move forward on the board, make the sound of the letters, or read the word, that you pass and land on.
5. For example, if a five comes up on the die, move five spaces on the game board and read five words and/or sounds.
6. If you land on "stop," remain on that circle for the duration of the turn. If you land on "clap," clap your hands and move forward a space. Otherwise, just keep moving as many places as the die shows.
7. The first person to reach the end wins.

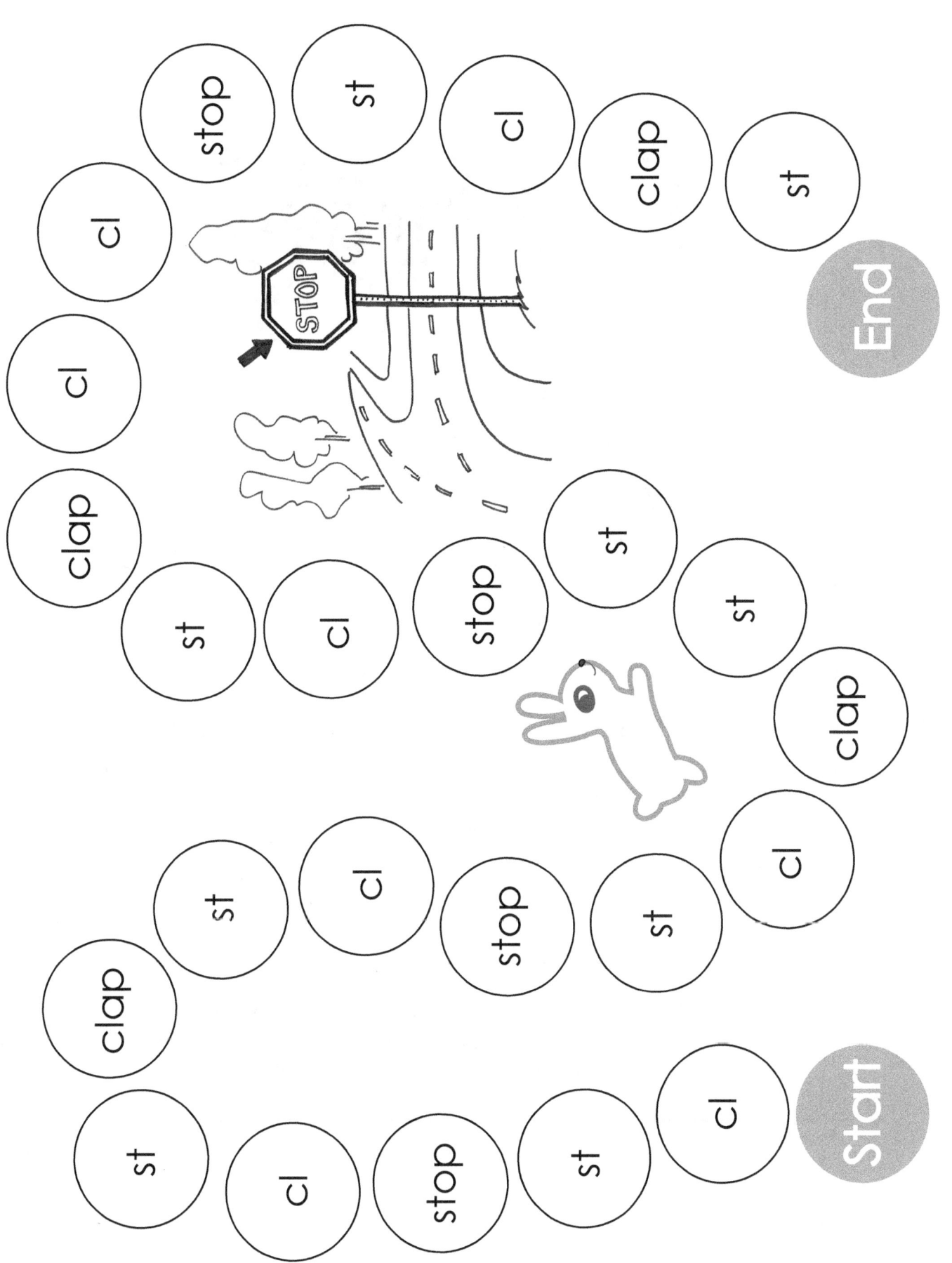

Step 10

Words that begin with...

sn-, sm-, sk-, sw-, sp-

Instructions

Say to the child: "**You did a great job learning how to read words that begin with sl-. Now you will learn words that begin with sn-, sm-, sk-, sw-, and sp-.**"

sn-, sp-, sk-, sm-, sw- words

Sound out ↓	Write the letter ↓	Write and read the word ↓
sn	s n ap	_ _ _ _
sp	__ot	_ _ _ _
sk	__in	_ _ _ _
sw	__im	_ _ _ _
st	__ack	_ _ _ _ _
sp	__ill	_ _ _ _ _
sm	__ell	_ _ _ _ _

Which word is it?

Say: "**Read each word out loud. Circle the word that goes with the picture.**"

Write the word and circle the picture

Say: "**Read the word out loud. Then write it, and circle the picture that shows the word.**"

spill

_ _ _ _ _

skip

_ _ _ _

swim

_ _ _ _

step

_ _ _ _

snack

_ _ _ _ _

stick

_ _ _ _ _

Draw a line from the word to the picture

Say: "**Read each word out loud.** Then draw a line from the correct word to the picture."

slim swim spin 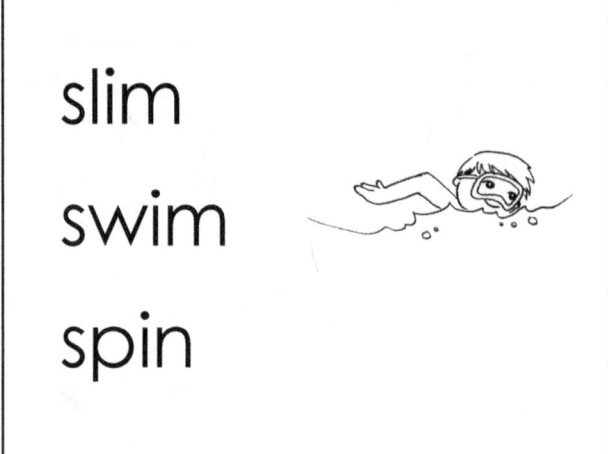	stop step stuff 
tick sick stick 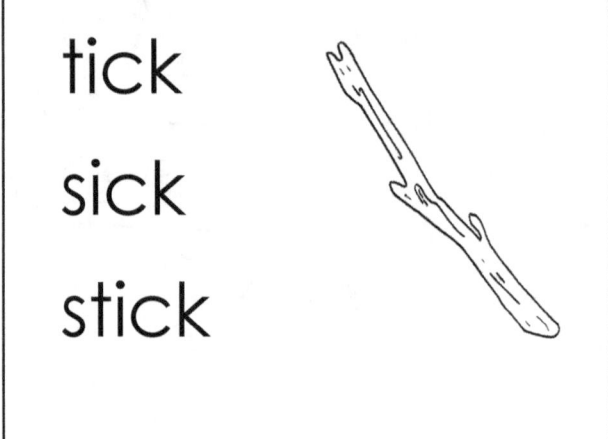	smell pill spill 
spell skip stick 	stuck sack snack 

Circle the letters

Say: **"Circle the correct letters. Then write the word."**
Tell the child the pictures show : slip, swim, skip, spill, twin, snack.

(s) m (l) p n (i) (p) t   s l i p

d s l w r i m g   _ _ _ _

h s o k i a t p   _ _ _ _

b t w l n i u n   _ _ _ _

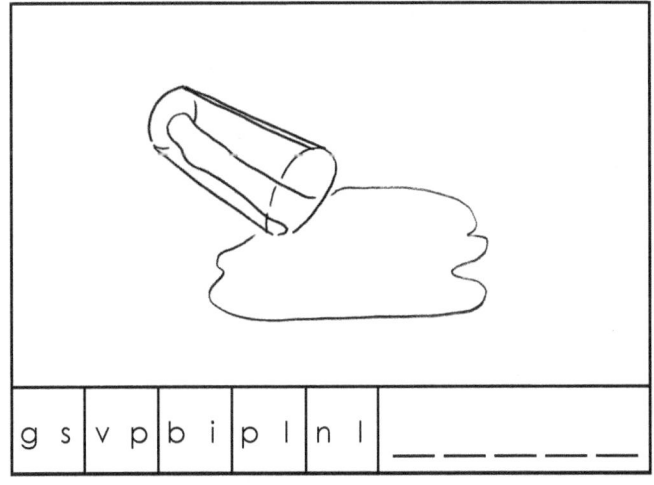

g s v p b i p l n l   _ _ _ _ _

g s v n i a c j n k   _ _ _ _ _

61

Step 11 — Power Word

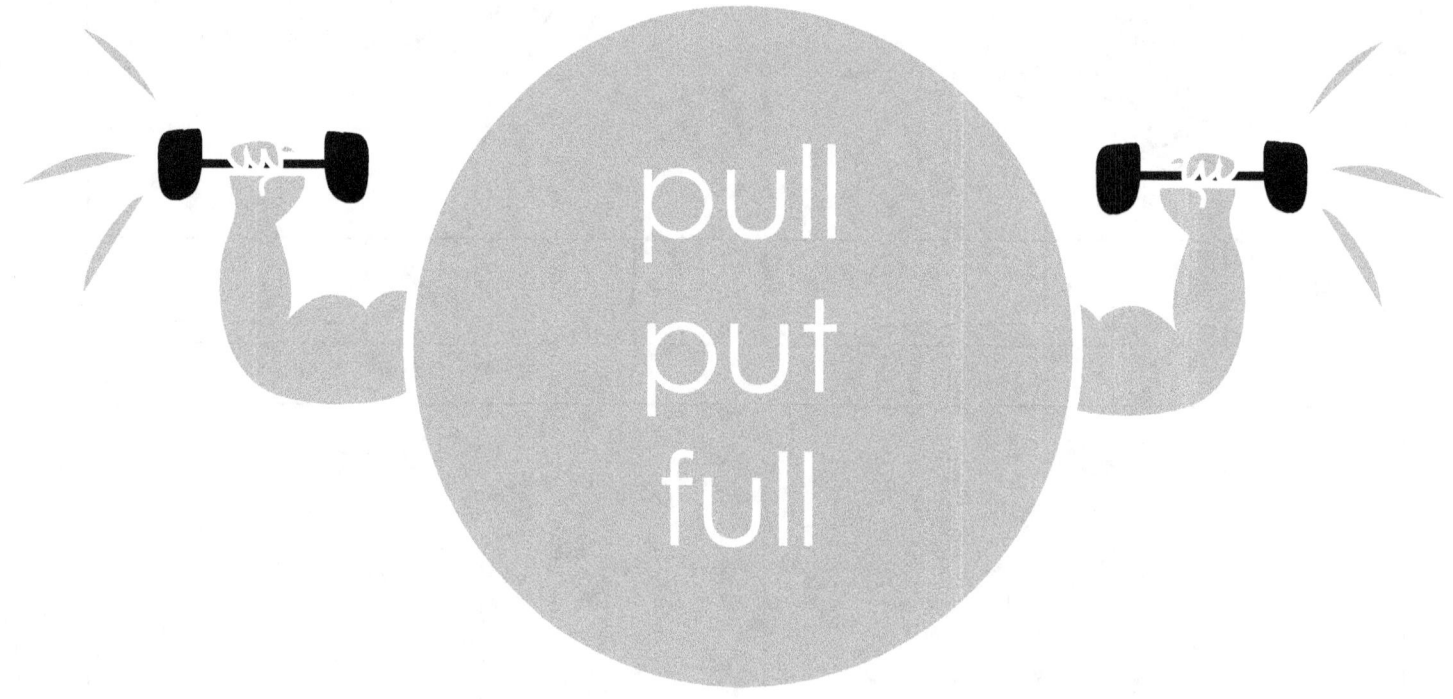

pull
put
full

Instructions

Point to the words "pull," "put," and "full," above. Say, "**These words are pull, put, and full** as in, `The boy will pull the wagon down the road,' or `The girl put away her games,' or `The child was full after dinner.'"

Write the Word

Say, "Trace the words 'pull,' 'put,' and 'full.' Then write them on the lines."

pull

put

full

pull

put

full

Does the sentence make sense?

Say: "**Read each sentence out loud. Color in the smiley face if the sentence makes sense, and the frown if it does not.**"

Put the snack in the box.	☺	☹
Bill did spill the full snack bag.	☺	☹
A duck can pull a sick clock.	☺	☹
Put the stick on the rack.	☺	☹
The cat will pull the full bag.	☺	☹
A dog can pull and spell.	☺	☹
Pull up on the step and stop.	☺	☹
A duck did put the spot on the log.	☺	☹

Read a book!

Instructions

Read a book

The child can now read the following books in the Alphabet Series. See Supplemental Materials," p. 1.

- Book 5: "Kim and Her Hat"
- Book 6: "Jam for Hap and Pam"
- Book 8: "Gum for a Pup"

Step 12

Words that begin with...

tr-, cr-, dr-, gr-, fr-

Instructions

Say to the child: "**You are doing so well! Now you're going to learn a whole new set of words. These words all have 'r' as their second letter. They are words like crab, truck, and drum.**"

Circle the letters

Say: "**Circle the letters at the beginning of the word the pictures show.**"
Tell the child the pictures show: truck, crib, crab, drum, frog, dress.

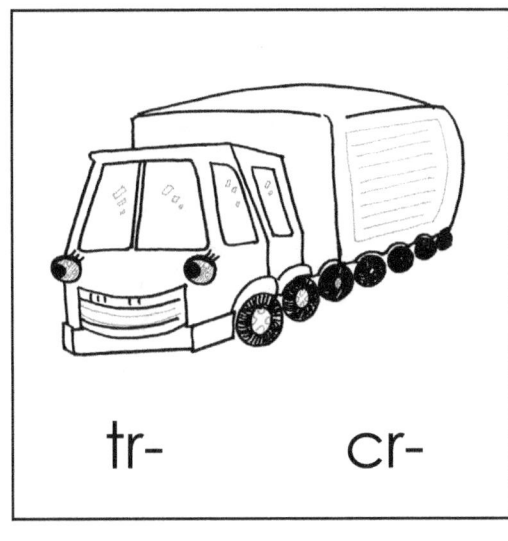

tr-   cr-

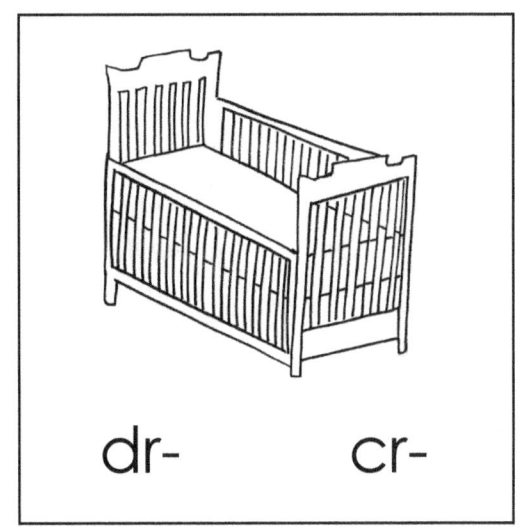

dr-   cr-

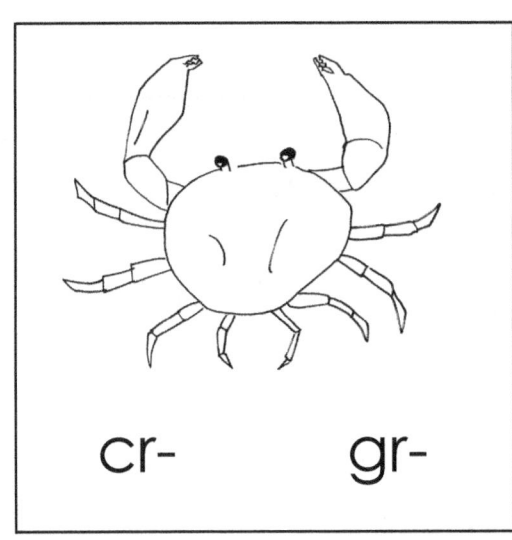

cr-   gr-

tr-   dr-

tr-   fr-

dr-   gr-

Which word is it?

Say: "**Read each word out loud. Circle the word that goes with the picture.**"

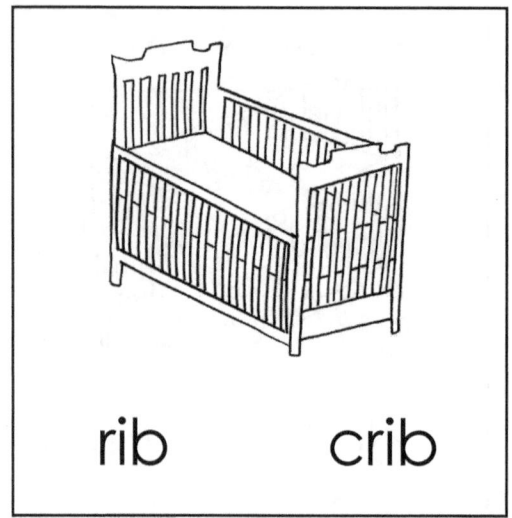

rib   crib

fog   frog

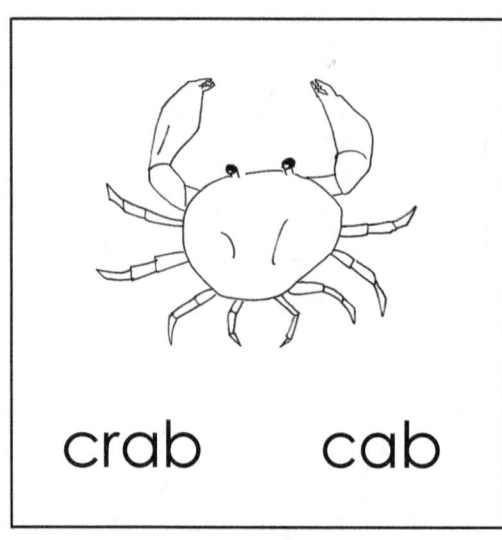

crab   cab

rink   drink

tuck   truck

press   dress

Write the word and circle the picture

Say: "**Read the word out loud. Then write it, and circle the picture that shows the word.**"

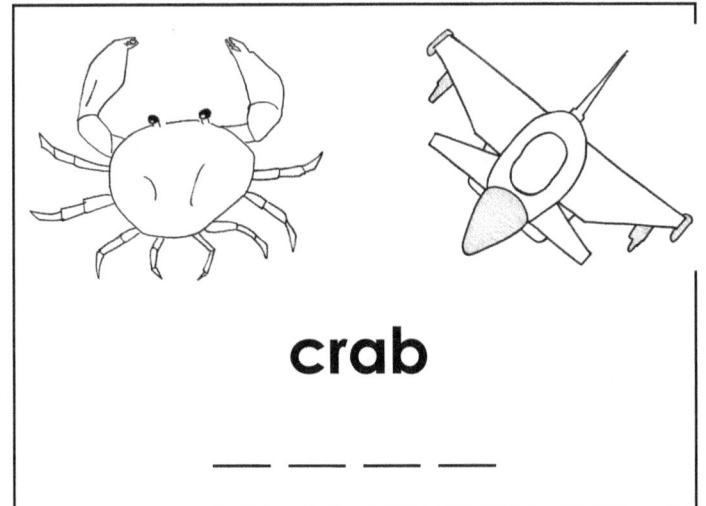

crab

_ _ _ _

drum

_ _ _ _

crib

_ _ _ _

truck

_ _ _ _ _

frog

_ _ _ _

drink

_ _ _ _ _

Draw a line from the word to the picture

Say: "**Read each word out loud. Then draw a line from the correct word to the picture.**"

cab
crab
crib

press
dress
stress

rink
drink
stink

snack
sack
snuck

still
pill
spill

tuck
truck
tick
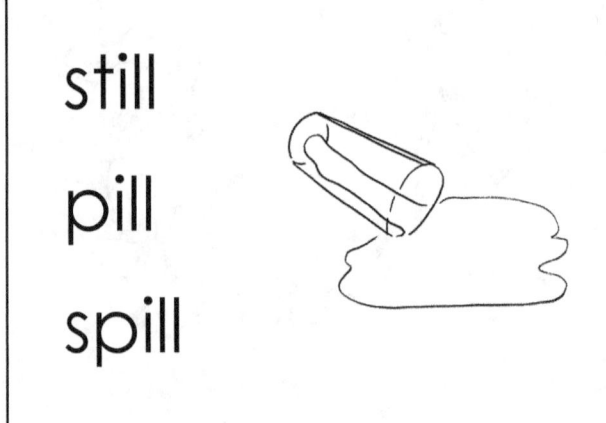

Circle the letters

Say: **"Circle the correct letters. Then write the word."**
Tell the child the pictures show: drum, frog, crib, crab, twin, truck.

| (d) | m | (r) | p | n | (u) | m | (t) | d r u m |

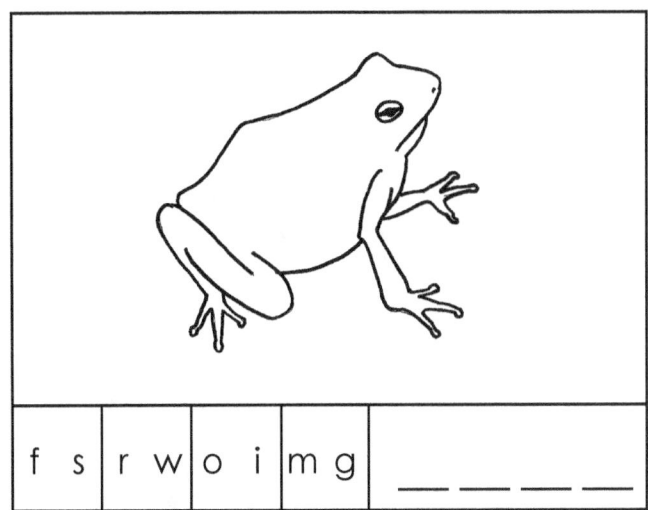

| f | s | r | w | o | i | m | g | _ _ _ _ |

| c | s | r | k | i | a | b | p | _ _ _ _ |

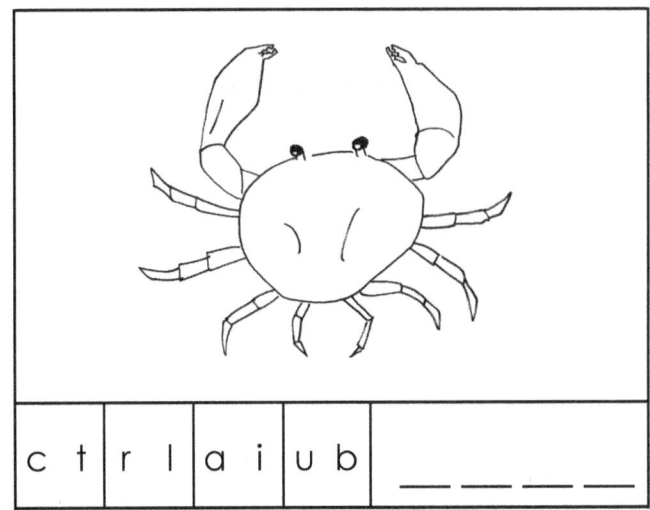

| c | t | r | l | a | i | u | b | _ _ _ _ |

| t | s | w | k | i | a | b | n | _ _ _ _ |

| t | s | r | n | i | u | c | j | n | k | _ _ _ _ _ |

71

Play a board game!

Instructions

Materials you will need:
- A single die.
- Coins to use as markers.
- Gameboard, *opposite page*.

1. Each player places a coin on "start."
2. Take turns rolling the die.
3. Move forward the same amount of spaces as the number on the die.
4. As you move forward on the board, read the words that you pass and land on.
5. For example, if a five comes up on the die, move five spaces on the game board and read five words.
6. The first person to reach the end wins.

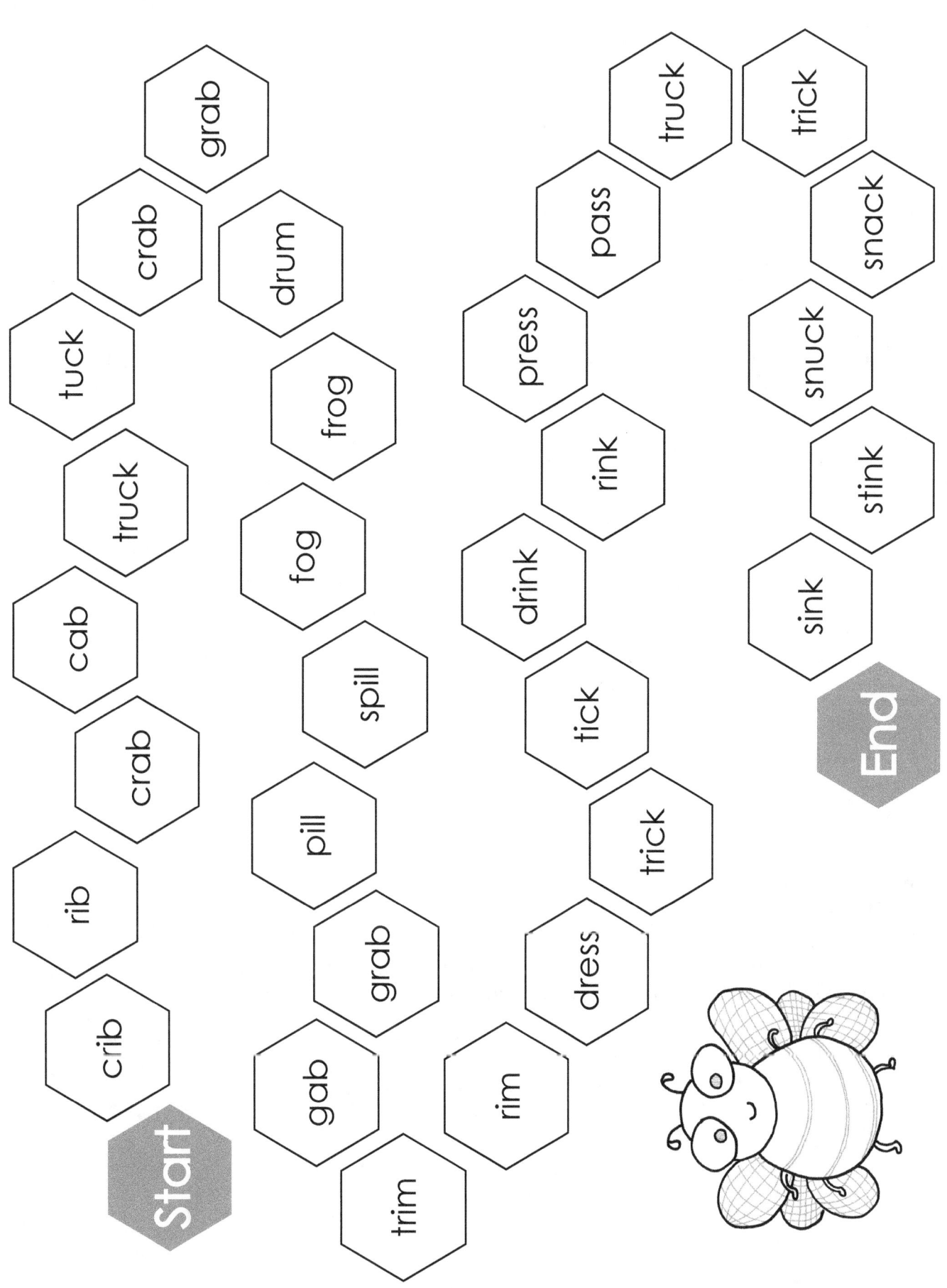

Step 13   Power Word

Instructions

Point to the word "little," *above.* Say, **"This word is `little,' as in, `The little cat followed its owner into the house,' or `I would like to drink a little water.'"**

Write the Word

Say, "**Trace the word 'little.' Then write it next to the one you traced.**"

75

Does the sentence make sense?

Say: "**Read each sentence out loud. Color in the smiley face if the sentence makes sense, and the frown if it does not.**"

The cat will trick the man.

A little crab can drag a drum.

The little frog is stuck on the stick.

A little crab did grab the big truck.

Tuck in the little pig in the crib.

The little frog did press the dress.

The man can trim the grass a little.

The little crab did spill the drink.

Read a book!

Instructions

Read a book

The child can now read:

- "Crab Trap." This is book 6 in the "Animal Antics" set by Nora Gaydos.
- "Ducks in Muck," by Lori Haskins.

See "Supplemental Materials," p. 1.

Play Beginning Blends Bingo

Instructions

Materials:
- Flashcards. Cut out the cards on the opposite page.
- 2 gameboards follow the flashcards. In Bingo, every player gets his or her own gameboard. You and the child should each select a gameboard to use.
- Pennies to use as game pieces.

1. Place the flashcards in one stack, with the words facing up.
2. Have the child read the word on the top card in the stack.
3. Each of you should look for that word on your Bingo boards and place a penny on top of the word on your boards when you find it.
4. Place the card the child read face down on the table.
5. Repeat steps 2-4. The child should be the one doing all of the reading of the words on the flashcards. Continue until one of you has five pennies in a row, either horizontally, vertically, or diagonally. The first player to get five in a row should call out, "Bingo!" That player wins the game.

Play Bingo!

sled	glass	grab	spot

smell	track	dress	crab	drip
snap	press	glad	frog	drink
brick	clock	drop	trick	plum
swim	sniff	spill	twig	small

This page is intentionally left blank.

This page is intentionally left blank.

BINGO

spot	track	dress	snap	drink
glass	press	brick	plum	sled
drip	clock	✗	glad	drop
sniff	frog	grab	trick	small
swim	smell	twig	crab	spill

BINGO

glad	sled	glass	grab	spot
smell	track	dress	crab	drip
snap	press	✕	frog	drink
brick	clock	drop	trick	plum
swim	sniff	spill	twig	small

This page is intentionally left blank.

Congratulations!

Instructions

Say: "**Congratulations!**

"**You now know how to read all the words that start with beginning blends.**

"**You should be very proud of yourself!**

"**I am very proud of you! You are doing such a great job.**"

Step 14   Ending Blends

Instructions

Say to the child: "**Wow! You've reached a whole new step in reading!**

"**The words in this lesson have two consonants at the end of the word. Each of those consonants will make its own sound.**"

Words that end in 'nd'

Words that end in...

nd

Instructions

Say to the child: "**Look at the pictures below. They show how adding just one letter makes a whole new word!**"

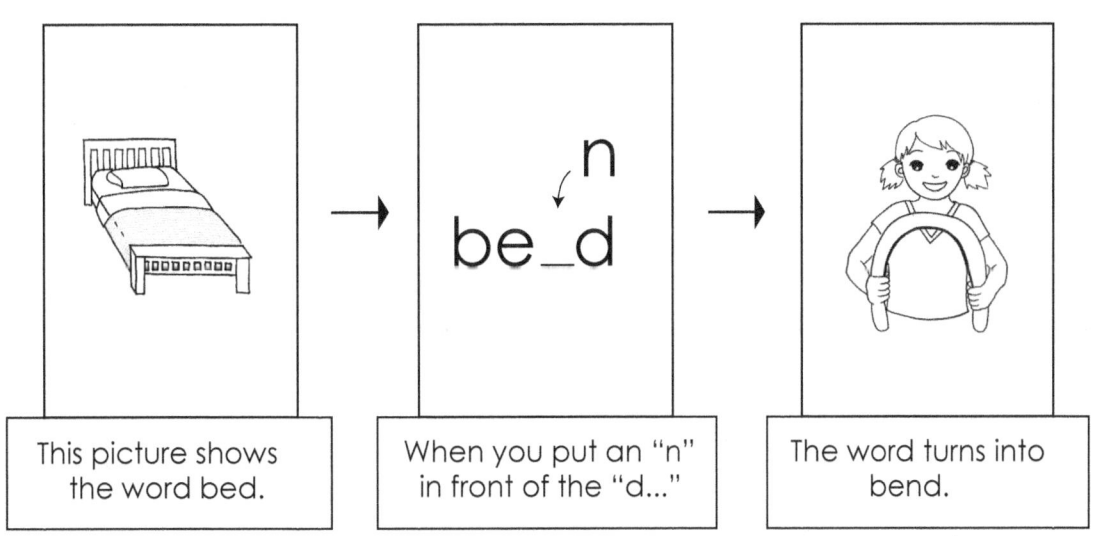

This picture shows the word bed.

When you put an "n" in front of the "d..."

The word turns into bend.

Words that end in -and

Write "and" on the blank lines ↓	Write and read the word ↓
b_and_	b a n d
s ___	___ ___
l ___	___ ___
h ___	___ ___
gr ___	___ ___
st ___	___ ___
br ___	___ ___

Words that end in -end

Write "end" on the blank lines ↓	Write and read the word ↓
b <u>end</u>	<u>bend</u>
s ___	___ ___
l ___	___ ___
m ___	___ ___
t ___	___ ___

Play the –and/–end board game

Instructions

Materials you will need:
- A single die.
- Coins to use as markers.
- Gameboard, *opposite page*.

1. Each player places a coin on "start."
2. Take turns rolling the die.
3. Move forward the same amount of spaces as the number on the die.
4. As you move forward on the board, read the words that you pass and land on.
5. For example, if a five comes up on the die, move five spaces on the game board and read five words.
6. The first person to reach the end wins.

Step 15 — Power Word

with

with

with

with

with

Does the sentence make sense?

Say: "**Read each sentence out loud. Color in the smiley face if the sentence makes sense, and the frown if it does not.**"

The pig did go with the band.	☺	☹

The dog did stand on the sand.	☺	☹

The man did stand with the crab.	☺	☹

The duck did land on the sand.	☺	☹

A crab did mend the dress.	☺	☹

The dog did lend the duck a hand.	☺	☹

Read a book

The child can now read "A Truck Can Help" by Judy Kentor Schmauss. See "Supplemental Materials," p. 1.

93

Step 16

Words that end in...

-mp or **-nk**

| Instructions |

Say to the child: "**Now you're going to learn to read words that end in 'mp' or 'nk.'**"

Circle the letters

Say: " **Circle the letters at the end of the word the picture shows.**"
Tell the child the pictures show: camp, dump, stamp, lamp, tank, skunk.

-nk   -mp

-mp   -nk

-mp   -nk

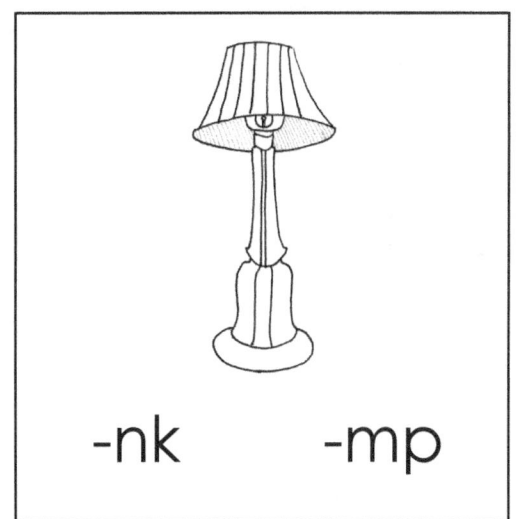

-nk   -mp

-nk   -mp

-mp   -nk

Write and read the word

Write "n" and "k" on the blank lines ↓	Write and read the word ↓
i n k	i n k
si _ _	_ _ _ _
wi _ _	_ _ _ _
pi _ _	_ _ _ _
ba _ _	_ _ _ _
ta _ _	_ _ _ _
sa _ _	_ _ _ _
bli _ _	_ _ _ _ _

Which word is it?

Say: "**Read each word out loud. Circle the word that goes with the picture.**"

lamp   stamp

skunk   sunk

lamp   hand

tank   bank

cramp   camp

damp   dump

Write and read the word

Write "m" and "p" on the blank lines ↓	Write and read the word ↓
la m p	l a m p
ca _ _	_ _ _ _
ra _ _	_ _ _ _
lu _ _	_ _ _ _
du _ _	_ _ _ _
sta _ _	_ _ _ _ _
stu _ _	_ _ _ _ _

Draw a line from the word to the picture

Say: "**Read each word out loud. Then draw a line from the correct word to the picture.**"

lamp
ramp
camp

bank
tank
rank

pump
bump
dump

ramp
camp
stamp

skunk
stink
stick

clamp
ramp
stamp

Write the word and circle the picture

Say: "Read the word out loud. Then write the word, and circle the picture that shows the word."

lamp

— — — —

dump

— — — —

damp

— — — —

camp

— — — —

stamp

— — — — —

skunk

— — — — —

Circle the letters

Say: "**Circle the correct letters. Then write the word.**"
Tell the child the pictures show: camp, dump, tank, lamp, stamp, skunk.

| (c) | m | r | (a) | n | (m) | (p) | c a m p |

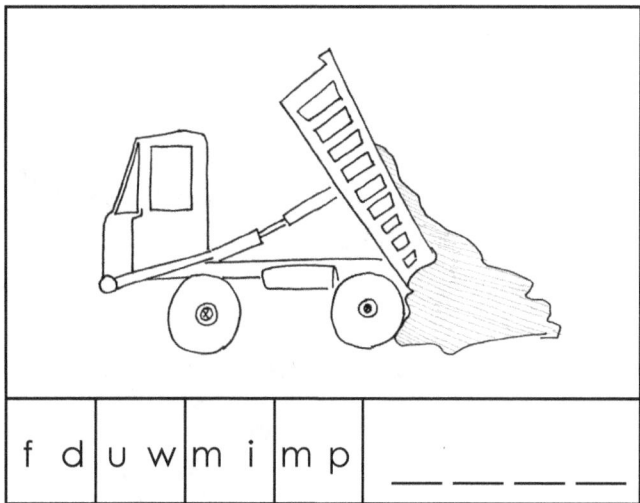

| f | d | u | w | m | i | m | p | _ _ _ _ |

| c | t | a | k | i | n | k | p | _ _ _ _ |

| c | l | a | l | a | m | u | p | _ _ _ _ |

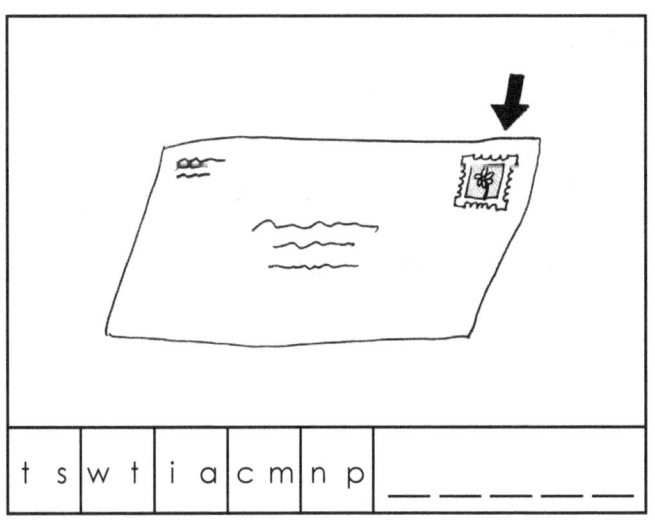

| t | s | w | t | i | a | c | m | n | p | _ _ _ _ _ |

| s | n | w | k | i | u | c | n | n | k | _ _ _ _ _ |

101

Play the -mp/-nk board game

Instructions

<u>Materials you will need</u>:
- A single die.
- Coins to use as markers.
- Gameboard, *opposite page*.

1. Each player places a coin on "start."
2. Take turns rolling the die.
3. Move forward the same amount of spaces as the number on the die.
4. As you move forward on the board, read the words that you pass and land on.
5. For example, if a five comes up on the die, move five spaces on the game board and read five words.
6. The first person to reach the end wins.

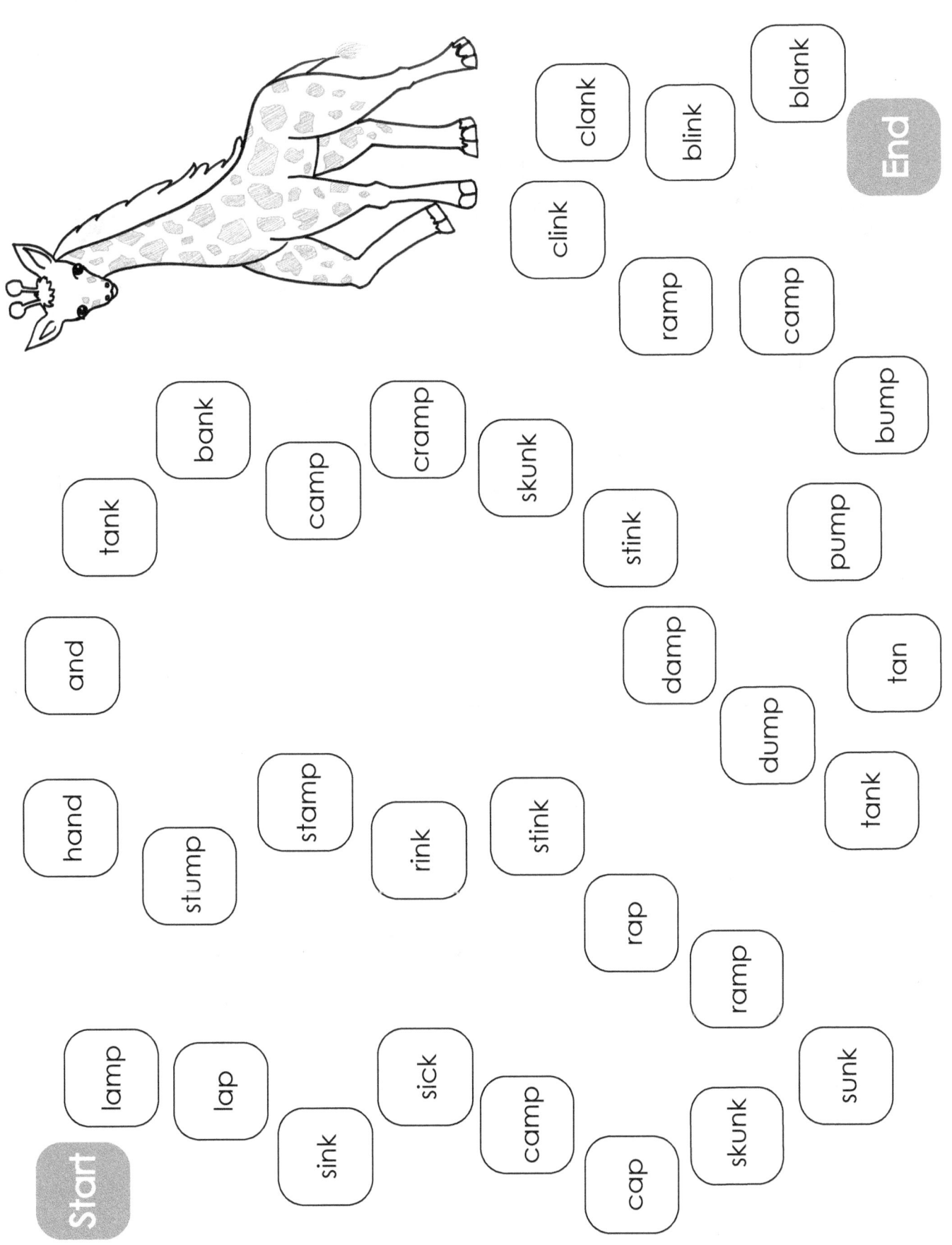

Step 17 　　　　　　　　　　　　　　　　　Power Word

look

look

look

look

Does the sentence make sense?

Say: "**Read each sentence out loud. Color in the smiley face if the sentence makes sense, and the frown if it does not.**"

Sentence	😊 ☹
A cat did look and blink.	
Look! The dump truck went up the ramp.	
The crab did look at the book.	
Look! The stamp is on the damp skunk.	
A skunk did look in the tank.	
Look! A crab did jump on the bed!	
The glass did clink and clank.	

Read a book

The child can now read the following two books in the "Animal Antics" set.

- Book 9: "Stuck Duck"
- Book 4: "Rub-a-Dub-Cub"

105

Step 18

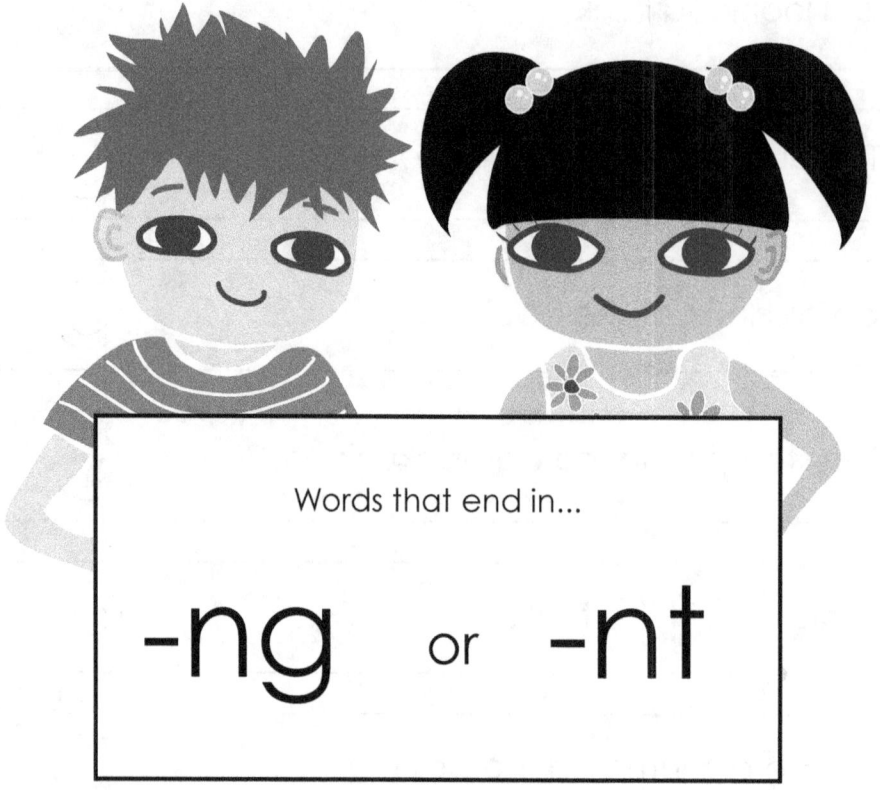

Words that end in...

-ng or -nt

Instructions

Say to the child: "**Now you're going to learn to read words that end in 'ng' or 'nt.'**"

-ng or -nt at the end?

Say: " **Circle the letters at the end of the word the pictures show.**"
Tell the child the pictures show: ring, hang, tent, bang, bent, sing.

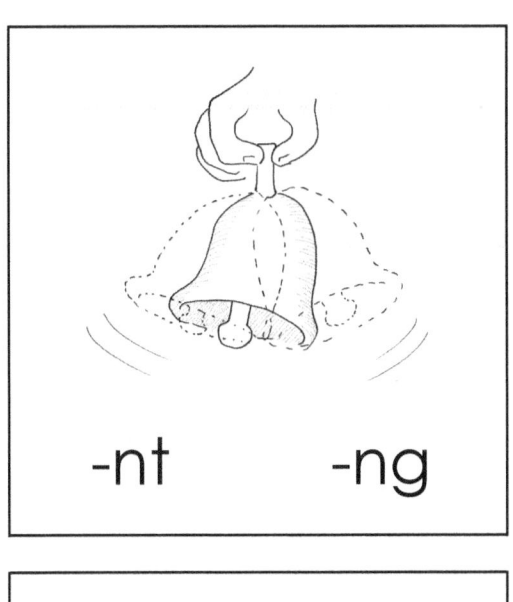

-nt   -ng

-ng   -nt

-ng   -nt

-nt   -ng

-ng   -nt

-nt   -ng

Write and read the word

Write "n" and "g" on the blank lines	Write and read the word
ki _n_ _g_	_k_ _i_ _n_ _g_
ba _ _	_ _ _ _
bri _ _	_ _ _ _ _
ha _ _	_ _ _ _
ri _ _	_ _ _ _ _
ra _ _	_ _ _ _
si _ _	_ _ _ _

Which word is it?

Say: "**Read each word out loud. Circle the word that goes with the picture.**"

rang   ring

king   sing

hand   hang

tent   ten

bang   clang

bring   sing

Write and read the word

Write "n" and "t" on the blank lines	Write and read the word
be n t	b e n t
de __ __	__ __ __ __
le __ __	__ __ __ __
re __ __	__ __ __ __
se __ __	__ __ __ __
te __ __	__ __ __ __
we __ __	__ __ __ __

Write the word and circle the picture

Say: **"Read the word out loud. Then write the word, and circle the picture that shows it."**

hang

___ ___ ___ ___

sing

___ ___ ___ ___

king

___ ___ ___ ___

bent

___ ___ ___ ___

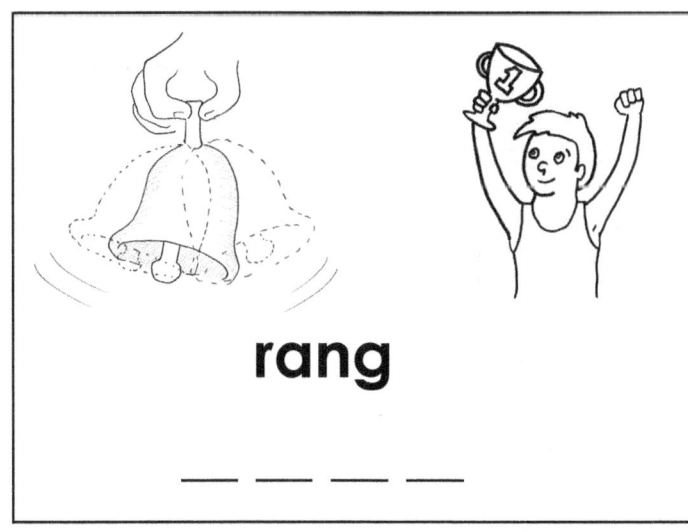

rang

___ ___ ___ ___

bang

___ ___ ___ ___

Draw a line from the word to the picture

Say: "Read each word out loud. Then draw a line from the correct word to the picture."

bang
clang
rang

sang
sing
bring

hand
hang
band
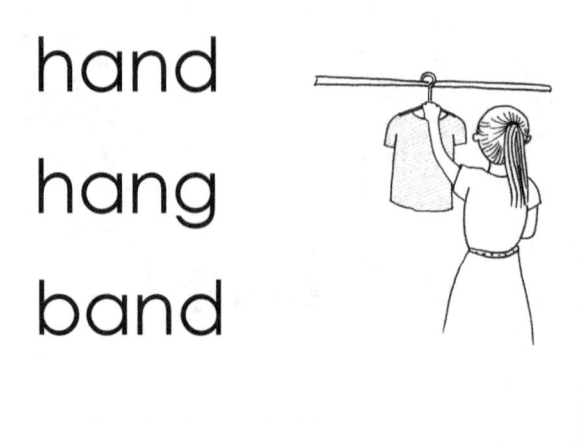

ring
rang
sing

ten
tent
rent

fling
bring
king

Circle the letters

Say: "**Circle the correct letters. Then write the word.**"
   Tell the child the pictures show : king, sing, bang, hang, bent, tent.

k m r i x n m g   k i n g

f s i w n i g p   _ _ _ _

b t a k i n k g   _ _ _ _

h l a l a n g p   _ _ _ _

b c a e m n k t   _ _ _ _

h t a e s n g t   _ _ _ _

Play Ending Blends Bingo

Instructions

<u>Materials</u>:
- Flashcards. Cut out the cards on the opposite page.
- 2 gameboards follow the flashcards. In Bingo, every player gets his or her own gameboard. You and the child should each select a gameboard to use.
- Pennies to use as game pieces.

1. Place the flashcards in one stack, with the words facing up.
2. Have the child read the word on the top card in the stack.
3. Each of you should look for that word on your Bingo boards and place a penny on top of the word on your boards when you find it.
4. Place the card the child read face down on the table.
5. Repeat steps 2-4. The child should be the one doing all of the reading of the words on the flashcards. Continue until one of you has five pennies in a row, either horizontally, vertically, or diagonally. The first player to get five in a row should call out, "Bingo!" That player wins the game.

Play Bingo!

	wing	camp	king	blink
skunk	rent	ring	sand	tank
dump	bank	tent	lamp	hang
bang	ramp	bring	sing	bend
sang	band	wink	stamp	fling

This page is intentionally left blank.

This page is intentionally left blank.

BINGO

tent	wing	camp	king	blink
skunk	rent	ring	sand	tank
dump	bank	✗	lamp	hang
bang	ramp	bring	sing	bend
sang	band	wink	stamp	fling

BINGO

blink	skunk	ring	dump	tank
bang	tent	ramp	hang	bring
camp	fling	✗	wing	bend
rent	lamp	sand	sang	band
sing	bank	stamp	king	wink

This page is intentionally left blank.

Step 19 Power Word

said

said

said

said

Does the sentence make sense?

Say: "**Read each sentence out loud. Color in the smiley face if the sentence makes sense, and the frown if it does not.**"

The duck did bring the pig a ring.	☺	☹

The man said, "Go in the tent."	☺	☹

Bring the king a bell to ring.	☺	☹

The man said the pig bent the lamp.	☺	☹

The cat did bang the drum and sing.	☺	☹

"I will drink the milk," said the cat.	☺	☹

Hang the dress on the stand.	☺	☹

The man said the dog sang a song.	☺	☹

Read a book!

Instructions

Read a book

The child can now read the following books in the "Animal Antics" set by Nora Gaydos. See "Supplemental Materials," p. 1.

- Book 3: "Pig Jigs"
- Book 5: "Wet Legs"
- Book 10: "Elk Yelps"

Power Word review

These are the Power Words the child has learned in this book.
Have the child read them to you to make sure he or she has mastered them.

see	down	little
says	put	with
go	pull	look
no	full	said

Congratulations!

You've completed Step 2 in reading!

Certificate of Accomplishment

Presented to _____

Signed: _____

Date: _____